The Lillie Enclave North End Fulham London

Bricks and Structures

from Over

Two Centuries

tell their own Story

Elizabeth Corwin

First published 2024
© 2024 Elizabeth Corwin

All rights reserved. No part of this publication may be reproduced, stored in a retrieval system, or transmitted by any means, electronic, mechanical, photocopying, recording or otherwise, without the prior written permission of the copyright holder and publishers.

ISBN 978 1 84674 431 0

Cover: Shell carving of Young & Son Architects, courtesy of www.londonremembers.com

Published by Countryside Books, Newbury
Produced by The Letterworks Ltd., Reading
Typeset by Linda Wade Design

Contents

Foreword by David Wardrop	5
Introduction	7
History	12
The heritage of the Lillie Enclave	17
The case for conserving Empress Place and shop parade	23
Its Architect	
Residents	
Enclave movers and shakers	26
Rus in Urbe	43
Legacy	44
Enclave burials at Brompton Cemetery	53
Afterword by Mark Balaam	53
Acknowledgements	55
Bibliography	57
Index	60
Picture credits	63

Above: Lansdown Terrace: 21-41 Lillie Road, south side, c 1960 (demolished). Courtesy 'Olney Collection', Hammersmith and Fulham archives

Below: Lillie Road, north side, with Hermitage cottages, Nos 62-64 on left and John Young terrace, Nos. 28-60, 2018

Foreword

Every family has its chronicler, the first person we call when we need to know about ourselves and where we came from. At the same time, heavy tomes weigh down our bookshelves, explaining our world, our country, and our borough. And that is where it tends to end, leaving a gap. So how do we drill down further, to our streets, their corners and crossings, unexplained patches of open ground, those buildings that shout out 'What was I once?'

This fascinating monograph by Elizabeth Corwin, a long-time local resident, shows how that gap in local knowledge can be filled, with attention to detail and filled with affection. And it is this affection for the Lillie Enclave at the north end of Fulham that shines through, introducing us to a rich history and vestiges that have borne witness to change.

In this age when an appalling lack of accommodation forces young renters to move onwards without settling, how can they possibly identify with our neighbourhood? For those more anchored here, we can recall that Pie and Mash shop in the North End Road, the clip-clop of the totter's cart with the shout of 'Any old iron!', the arrival and then the demolition of Earls Court 2, and the transformation of the Empress State Building.

But even those with long memories can only reminisce so far. This work provides us with so much more, bringing us stories right back to the eighteenth century. It has no didactic mission to explain. Instead, it invites us to take a walk through our neighbourhood and, as we go, it points to this and to that, answering questions such as 'why' and 'how' and 'does it matter', with charm and affection.

I know you will enjoy it

     David Wardrop
     London 2024

Above: Empress Place in 2019 is the backdrop to developments in the Enclave
Below: The west side of Empress Place in the 1960s

Introduction

Will this monograph turn out to be a history or an obituary?

This story sets out the case for the full retention of the Lillie Enclave in north-east Fulham and its sensitive integration within the Earls Court redevelopment.

The purpose of this work is to alert the reader to the connections that abound here and to why demolition, proposed by an ambitious regeneration scheme, matters. Here is a remarkable heritage site in West London, identified as the Lillie Enclave, whose remaining Regency and Victorian structures have borne witness, for over 200 years and with some grace, to an ongoing story of grand projects, speculators, architects, brewers, sportsmen, engineers and consultants. Some of them did indeed leave an indelible mark on history, especially in the few ornate buildings extant, the railways, transport, automotive and entertainment industries. 2024 is another historic planning juncture when the Enclave could have a whole arm amputated and leave the perception of private and public thoroughfares confused.

John Young's 16 Lillie Road in 1970

The Lillie Enclave is named after Sir John Scott Lillie and covers the cruciform road layout he made across his land in the 1820s to facilitate public access to the Kensington Canal, now a railway, and to link the public roads of ancient Fulham with Brompton. The remaining part of the Enclave now in the balance comprises the historic Empress Place and 2-26 Lillie Road SW6, a mid-Victorian residential and retail development still extant, along with Lillie Bridge, on two arms of Lillie's original layout. All these structures are facing complete obliteration in a bid for

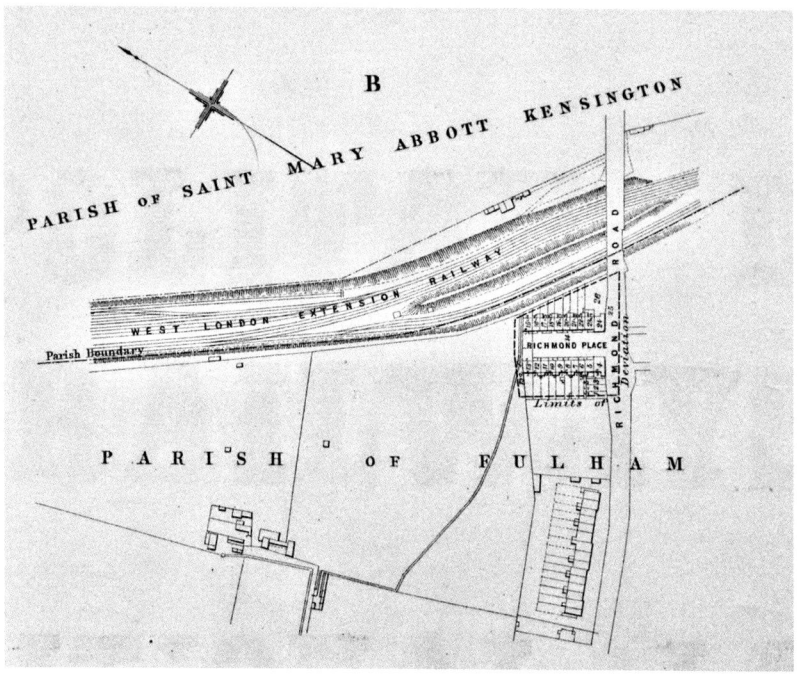

Above: John Fowler's 1868 plan showing the former Richmond (now Empress) Place development and nos. 2 to 26 and 30 to 58 Richmond (now Lillie) Road, in preparation for the 1869 Session of Parliament with a request to permit further railway works on the parish boundary
Courtesy of London Metropolitan Archives

regeneration. What follows offers, it is to be hoped, a clear case for their conservation.

Just three unremarked streets on the edge of the former Middlesex village of North End, in today's Fulham, prove to have more hidden heritage than meets the busy eye. First, is the top end of Lillie Road, a somewhat notorious trunk road associated with the back entrance to the now demolished international Earls Court[2] exhibition Centre - just over the notable Lillie Bridge - itself now at risk of obliteration. They are an actual historical link between the Enclave, its structures and activities with the unique Brompton Cemetery and West Brompton station, which also straddles parish and borough boundaries.

Introduction

Second is Seagrave Road, to the south, with a narrow entrance and a few small shops, including the Atlas public house (1869). Further down is an ambulance station and, at the end, past Victorian and 20th-century low-rise homes, dwarfed by facing bold glass and steel 21st-century apartment buildings, is the London Oratory School (est. 1863), which relocated here in 1970. Who could now surmise that buried under some of the modern steel and glass structures here, are the footprints of thousands of sportspeople, later replaced by the tyre prints of the celebrated marques I call the 'Three Rs': Rolls Royce, Renault and Rover? All of them had their London depots here, the final one until the 1970s, so close to the then 'Motor Show' venue.

Third to the north, is the vestige of a once symmetrical and well-proportioned broad Mid-Victorian cul-de-sac, Empress Place, originally Richmond Place, a characterful display of architecture in an era of transition. Shortly before World War II, radical redevelopment by Watney's Brewery of *The Prince of Wales Tavern*, one of two symmetrical corner buildings, at the entrance into Empress Place from Lillie Road, breached the street's harmonious layout, by demolishing three neighbouring houses in Empress Place to expand. As a result, the street was renumbered and lost some of its intended symmetry in the cause of commerce. The street became a planning and conservation orphan, clinging to the pleasing charm afforded it by its highly original but long-forgotten designer.

---

[2] The name of the eponymous former exhibition centre in Earl's Court is spelt without an apostrophe. It is anomalous because the area in which it stood once belonged to several Earls of Oxford, but the centre itself never did thus allowing its creators to adopt a more simplified form of modern spelling. See for example Phil Soar on https://exhibitionnews.uk/exhibitions-vital-questions-demanding-answers.

These three streets played host to an extraordinary range of people and activity over the past two hundred years - arguably a microcosm of the Industrial Revolution - and the verve associated with urbanisation. The movers and shakers who alighted here contributed to

- Aircraft construction
- Arts and music
- Automotive engineering
- Brewing, distilling and wine-making
- Civil and defence planning
- Design and building trades
- Education
- Entertainment
- Food production
- Health services
- Music recording
- Refugee reception
- Sporting prowess
- Telecommunications
- Transport and engineering

The people who have added to the vibrancy of the Lillie Enclave came initially from rural parts of England, but also from abroad, such as the 18th-century Florentine engraver, Francesco Bartolozzi or the Hungarian impresario, Imre Kiralfy in the 1880s. Then there were the Americans, especially, the Oglala Sioux from South Dakota, performing for Buffalo Bill (William Cody), as did Annie Oakley. They were followed by mass transport entrepreneurs, Charles Yerkes, Albert Stanley and the estimable theatre architect C. Howard Crane from Detroit. Among other Europeans we should note the contemplative

Belgian nuns who settled in 1880 for about 30 years, then several thousand Belgian refugees fleeing World War I, put up in the capacious Empress Hall. More recently, for it was in 1979, a young Hans Zimmer came from Germany to launch his now Oscar studded musical career in a recording studio he conjured at the bottom of a yard. Perhaps others will come to light in the future.

Another feature which is almost gone is the local biodiversity. By happenstance, the green littoral of Counter's Creek and Kensington Canal became the rich verges of the railway lines, enriched by ballast likely brought in from the South Downs.

It benefited from the adjoining Brompton Cemetery, whose flora has lain largely undisturbed since it was fields in the early 19th century. Little heed has been paid to the flora and fauna clinging on in the Lillie Enclave, as bulldozers and then landscape contractors impose themselves on the heritage 💷

---------------- History ----------------

The scattered village of North End in the ancient Parish of Fulham, bordered by Counter's Creek and the Parish of Kensington beyond, was home to a number of notable people in the 18th and 19th centuries, who had settled in this part of the county of Middlesex. One of the grand houses in the area was 'The Hermitage' with its 15-acre estate. It stood, until after WW1, on land east of today's junction of the North End and Lillie Roads, all the way up to Lillie Bridge. Among its proprietors was the actor and dramatist, Samuel Foote (1720-1777) of Panjandrum fame and later, the decorated Peninsular War veteran, Sir John Scott Lillie (1790-1868), born in County Roscommon, soldier, entrepreneur, inventor and Whig activist supporter of statesman Daniel O'Connell MP as well as being a published scourge of parliamentary corruption. He was an early antivivisectionist and recipient of a humanitarian medal for saving a small boy from drowning in the Thames.

Above: The Hermitage, North End, ca. 1772, unknown artist, eighteenth century, Oil on canvas, Yale Center for British Art, Paul Mellon Collection, B1993.30.5. Westminster Abbey is depicted to the right on the horizon.

History

Above left: Samuel Foote (1720-1777) Above right: Sir John Scott Lillie, © NPG Photo by Silvy

Above: 1871 Ordnance Survey map of North End showing Lillie Bridge and Lillie Road with Richmond Gardens (Empress Place) and Seagrave Road, Fulham Parish

'Richmond Place', later 'Empress Place' and the attached Mid-Victorian shops in Italianate style, fronting Richmond Road, later Lillie Road, were built in the early 1860s on the extreme end of what

13

had been the Hermitage estate. This was the result of parcelling up of the land and urbanisation following the saga of the Kensington Canal (1826), its huge basin and short-lived port on land which became the popular Lillie Bridge Sports Grounds (1866-1889) and the gradual development of the railway lines which replaced the ill-conceived canal project to connect the Grand Union Canal with the Thames following the littoral of Counter's Creek. Sir John Scott Lillie's legacy, as proprietor of the 'Hermitage' and shareholder of the Kensington Canal Co. and of the Hammersmith Bridge Co., was the creation on his land of a new and alternative road route from the village of Brompton via Lillie Bridge and Crown Lane to access Hammersmith Bridge. He also created two service roads for the canal port, today's Empress Place and Seagrave Road. He built a brewery and tavern, 'The Lillie Arms', now bowdlerised as the 'Lillie Langtry' Public House (1835). He also had erected two Late Georgian pairs of terraces, 62-64, 'Hermitage Cottages' and 'Rosa Cottages', 66-68 Lillie Road, now Grade II listed. The canal venture was late and ran out of money. Lillie eventually left the Enclave, named in his memory.

After many delays, take note, a series of companies and engineers managed to turn a watercourse into functioning railways, but not until the second half of the 19th century. This was the shot in the arm the Enclave needed. The fields were put into service for sport, engineering, international exhibitions and mass entertainment. This lasted for over a century.

The Royal Family's association with Earls Court, began with Buffalo Bill's *Wild West*, part of the American Exhibition, during Queen Victoria's Jubilee Year in 1887. The shows they honoured with their presence included The Royal Tournament, the Smithfield Show, Boat Show, Motor Show, the ever-popular Ideal Home Show and various trade exhibitions. As a concert venue, and to a lesser extent a sports arena, the sixty years after World War II brought into Earls Court a roll call of top international performers. Earls Court a

---

[3] 1848 map in RBKC archives shows the service roads for the Kensington Canal on the Fulham Parish side.

History

roll call of top international performers.

The lesser-known names which feature in this story may nonetheless surprise the reader. Among the residents, entrepreneurs and practitioners in the *Lillie Enclave* were Adam Aaronson, Francesco Bartolozzi, Joseph Bickley, John Chambers, Sir John Fowler, W.G. Grace, Sir Geoffrey de Havilland, William Hurlstone, Imre Kiralfy, Henry Lovibond, Emmeline Pankhurst, Samuel Richardson, Charles Rolls (of Rolls Royce), John Robinson Whitley, John Young and as mentioned the feted, Hans Zimmer.

The prevalence of infectious diseases in London in the 1870s, led to the construction of a 500-bed hospital on 13 acres off Seagrave Road, while the injured of World War I attended the Fulham and Putney Orthopaedic Clinic at 16 Lillie Road. Prior to that, facing the Watney's tavern on the opposite corner, it had been a *Lockhart's Refreshment Rooms*, born out of the Temperance movement.

Myriad businesses and organisations, some of them remembered to this day, have been established within the Enclave in Fulham:

Airco (aircraft manufacture), the Amateur Athletics Association, Banham's Security, Beaufort House (Mental Asylum) and Beaufort House School, Belgian Refugee Reception Centre (Empress Hall, 1915), Burnett's White Satin Gin, Cannon's Brewery, the Civil Service Sports Club, Corbett and McClymont (of the Gunter estate), Belgian Discalced Carmelite Order for Women (at Hermitage Lodge), Domidium Interior Design, Earl's Court Pleasure Gardens, Edmonds & Co. (horticultural factors), The Empress Hall, replaced by the Empress State Building – referred to as 'ESB' by the Ministry of Defence and Metropolitan Police insiders – The Fulham and Putney Orthopaedic Clinic, Gander & White, (art logistics), The Great Northern, Piccadilly and Brompton Line, the Great Wheel (tallest ever Ferris wheel for the Empire of India exhibition 1894), Gregory, Bottley & Lloyd

Above: Just off 82 Lillie Road, the historic sign was stolen prior to the Covid pandemic

(minerals and fossils), Joseph Bickley (architectural modeller), Sir John Lillie's Brewery, Lillie Bridge (Railway) Depot, Lillie Bridge Sports Grounds, Lillie Hall (roller skating rink), 6, Lillie Yard recording studio (film music), Lockhart's Refreshment Rooms, London Ambulance Service station, London Cru (wine production), London Oratory School, the London Roadcar Co., the Kensington Canal Co., Marsh Bros. (electrical factors), the Metropolitan and District Line Railway, Middlesex County Cricket Club, (MCC), Midland Railway Goods and Coal Depot, XIV Olympiad, Peabody Estate, C.S Rolls' & Co. car dealership in Lillie Hall, Renault workshops (1908-1935), Rover Company (1935-1971), the 2nd South Middlesex Rifle Volunteers, Spaghetti House (fast food), Stewart's Garage, the 2nd South Middlesex Rifle Volunteers, Tanous, (Fine Art framers), Telfers Pies, Vickers' Gin, the West London Junction Railway, the Western Isolation hospital and the ZeST Gallery (studio glass blowing). All but a few are now gone. In 1950 the automated Fulham Telephone Exchange also came to Lillie Road, on the former Hermitage estate, in a narrow lane eponymously named Telephone Place ∭

Heritage of the Lillie Enclave

Above: Surviving Kensington Canal bridge arch (1826) beneath the Lillie Bridge

The extant heritage of this small area may be summarised as the Georgian-era road layout, four Late-Georgian houses, and two Mid-Victorian neighbouring clusters of mainly residential terraces with basements in Empress Place and along the north side of Lillie Road which were the work of one architect, John Young. In addition, there are the Italianate shop parade, the Victorian railway lines, the traction maintenance sheds at the Lillie Bridge Depot and part of the Grade II station along with a few related Regency, Victorian and Edwardian structures (16-18 Empress Place), of which more in the afterword at the end, plus one late Georgian public house and associated industrial building, on the southside of Lillie Road and Victorian clusters down Seagrave Road.

The Lillie Enclave, North End, Fulham, London

Above: Regency period steps onto Kensington Canal wharf at railside – 2014 Courtesy of Nick Woollven Below: The former 'Lillie Arms' (1835), now the 'Lillie Langtry' public house at 19 Lillie Road

Heritage of the Lillie Enclave

Above: Courtesy of Wellcome Collection: Wikimedia Commons, CC-BY-4.0 Below left: John Young's corner building in Lombardic-Gothic style 1861, at 23-25 Eastcheap. City of London. Copyright Stephen Richards Below right: Young's 1862 Italianate corner tavern 14 Lillie Road, prior to replacement by a neo-Arts and Crafts style in 1938

John Young and his firm

The pertinence of the *Royal Marsden Hospital*, originally the New Cancer Hospital in Fulham Road, to Empress Place and the Mid-Victorian terrace on the north side of Lillie Road may seem surprising, but it is that they were all authored by one practice, Messrs John Young & Son, owned by John Young (1797-1877), architect and surveyor for the City of London.

Above: John Young (1797-1877) architect and surveyor.
Photo by Maull. With permission of London Metropolitan Archive.

John Young's obituary in *The Builder* magazine, edited by the influential architect George Godwin, could not list all of his many projects and achievements; suffice to say, he was regarded as a 'safe pair of hands' by clients and colleagues alike. He moved in august architectural circles, starting with Porden, then Nash, Decimus Burton, Cubitt, as well as the Cundys and Vulliamy, among others.

In 1828, he was the author of an illustrated book *Shopfronts, Porticos and Entrances – A Series of Designs for Shop Fronts, Porticoes and Entrances to Buildings Public and Private* with engravings by Henry Adlard, published by Taylors Architectural Publishers of Holborn. Young's own busy and wide-ranging practice at 46 Clarges Street eventually included his own eldest son, John (1830-1910), a specialist in ecclesiastic structures, while assisted by other architects, most notably Frederick Hyde Pownall (1831-1907) and David Mocatta (1806-1882), a Sephardic Jew, known for designing several synagogues and distinguished buildings in Brighton.

The reason John Young came to Fulham to build 35 houses and shops, was probably opportunistic. Likely as not, his neighbour and brick supplier from Stoke Newington, Joseph Webb, had too many bricks left over after the New Cancer Hospital was completed in 1859. Their colleague, John Elger (1820-1889), master builder in nearby Brompton and speculative developer of Rutland Gate and Ennismore Gardens in Brompton, happened to own the sliver of land along Richmond Road and sold it on to Young and Webb for their two-part development[4]. The first part, begun in 1861, was to be two facing symmetrical terraces for residential occupation for newly arrived people benefiting from the railway into London, with parallel retail outlets on the north side of the main road up to Lillie Bridge. It was then named Richmond Place.

The second part was to be a terrace of 15 more spacious upmarket homes for the professional class, facing the Palladian villas, such as Lansdown Terrace, already erected in the 1840s, opposite in Richmond (later Lillie) Road. Young's 'upmarket' three-storey terrace with basements in Lillie Road, nos. 30-58 (even) have terracotta detailing with dogtooth panels, and nos. 30 and 58 have recessed porches. Nos. 28 and 60 end pavilions with canted bow windows to the first and second

Above: John Young's original no. 14 Richmond Place, (later 17 Empress Place), the only remaining double-fronted house in the street

---

[4] Several assignments of the houses in Richmond Place put beyond doubt that in 1866 John Young, architect and Joseph Webb, brick merchant, sold the freeholds to professional investors.

Above: Young's trade-mark polychromatic brickwork reprised on the Lillie Road terrace

floors. All are locally listed. The great give-away of this two-part project, (1861-1867), was Young's signature polychromatic brickwork, using terracotta and Suffolk-stone friezes. It is in effect a continuity of his practice designs on the New Cancer Hospital in Fulham Road, commented on by Edward Walford in 1878, (see British History Online https://www.british-history.ac.uk/old-new-london/vol5), and an echo of Young's Grade II listed warehouse building in Eastcheap, whose brick detail elicited architectural raptures from historians Bridget Cherry and Nikolaus Pevsner ᨇ

The Case for Conserving Empress Place

It is surely by omission that the earlier part of Young and Webb's project of two terraces of flat-fronted Mid-Victorian two-storey cottages with basements in Empress Place were not listed in 1993 when the local authority had the opportunity. The local authority only listed the three-storey John Young terrace in Lillie Road, failing to note that the two-storey cottages were historically and characteristically part of the one and the same project.

It's the poetry and the spirit of place that inspires the onlooker. This attractive small cul-de-sac, off the eastern end of today's Lillie Road was formerly known as Richmond Place/Gardens, a stone's throw from West Brompton station. It presents facing terraces of two storey cottages, variously up or down-graded over time. The rendered basements and ground-floors retain some uniformity with their dainty porticos. Where it is exposed, the interesting brickwork on the upper storeys, likewise reprised on 30-58 Lillie Road, has been smothered in paint or re-chiselled and extended according to the unsynchronised modest fashions of recent years. For years, it abutted the historic Lillie Bridge traction depot and Earl's Court Pleasure Gardens, later Earls Court Exhibition Centre. At the turn of the previous century, it gave access to Collard's 5,000-seater *Empress Hall*, replaced in 1961 by the Empress State Building, formerly leased by the Ministry of Defence, currently a Metropolitan Police asset, with nesting opportunities for kestrels, providing the railway verges afford them sufficient prey!

It owes its name to Queen Victoria, Empress of India, who broke her mourning for Prince Albert, when for her first public engagement in May 1887, she and her entourage attended the Buffalo Bill's *Wild West* spectacle in her Jubilee Year and used Richmond Gardens to access the venue for the American Exhibition and spectacular display. It featured Annie Oakley and included

First Nation performers, notably, Chief Sitting Bull and Chief Long Wolf of the Oglala Sioux. When Long Wolf died in 1892 during a subsequent tour in London, William Cody bought a burial plot for him in the local Brompton Cemetery where he rested for over a century,

Above left: Queen Victoria as Empress of India. Photo by Ostroróg aka Walery.
Above right: Annie Oakley, the sharp-shooter may have strolled along Empress Place on her way to a performance at The Earls Court venue

until his descendants were able to take his remains and those of four other Oglala deceased, home to South Dakota in 1997.

Residents of Richmond Gardens
Some of the first residents of Richmond Gardens, or Richmond Place, as Empress Place was formerly called, did not necessarily own the properties. They included an architect and surveyor, Frederick Tyerman, at no. 6; an artist, James Waylen, at no. 15; two surgeons, Mr Joseph Sewell at no. 2 and Mr Martin Hurlstone at no. 12. The latter was married to a musician, Maria Bessy Styche and in 1876 they became the parents of a musical prodigy, William Hurlstone (1876-1906), composer and pianist born in their house.

Sir Charles Stanford would later comment that William was the most gifted of his students at the Royal College of Music, who at that time included Frank Bridge, Gustav Holst, John Ireland, Ralph Vaughan Williams and Samuel Coleridge-Taylor, a life-long friend of Hurlstone's. It is likely that William's first works were composed at home in Richmond Gardens. Hurlstone became Professor of Harmony at the Royal College of Music and conductor of the Bach Choir. He lived in Croydon most of his short adult life and is buried in the local cemetery.

Above left: William Hurlstone (1876-1906), composer born at 12 Richmond Gardens Courtesy of Royal College of Music. Above right: (today's 14 Empress Place)

Latterly, the reader should note, despite having been outside the original regeneration masterplan, through determined acquisitions by the first development company on the project, residents and owners in Empress Place and 2–26 Lillie Road all vacated the premises. Most of the properties are curently occupied under 'meanwhile use' by retailers, charities or local artists. 🎵

Enclave Movers and Shakers[1]

Relatively close to the river Thames and the creeping western outskirts of London, the fields of North End and its neighbouring village of Walham Green (currently called Fulham Broadway) in the County of Middlesex - for during much of the 19th-century, here was still countryside - offered great scope for industry and urbanisation. In brief then, here are some of the other main actors in the history of the Lillie Enclave.

James Gunter (1731-1819), Chelsea landowner, Mayfair confectioner, builder of a timber footbridge over Counter's Creek circa 1760.

Lord Kensington, William Edwardes (1777-1855) MP for Haverford West, landowner, instigator of the Kensington Canal, 1822. It opened in 1828 but was a failure and in 1839 was sold to the Birmingham, Bristol and Thames Junction Railway Company (later the West London Railway).

Robert Gunter (1783-1852) son of James, builder of the first brick and stone bridge over the creek/canal (1826) – still visible from platform 4, West Brompton station and later owner of an orchard, known as 13a Richmond Place at the bottom of the present Empress Place.

Benjamin Rawlinson Faulkner (1787-1849), colonial official and society portrait painter lived in Hermitage Cottages, Lillie Road.

Miss Gosling, businesswoman. According to historian Charles Féret, she was the first person to run Lillie's North End brewery, behind the Lillie Arms.

Movers and Shakers in the Enclave

Above: The Kensington Canal circa 1845 marking the boundary between Kensington parish to the left with the newly laid out Brompton Cemetery and Fulham Parish and the 'Lillie Enclave' to the right

William Cutbush, Lord Kensington's surveyor and nominal 'engineer' of the Kensington Canal, basin and wharves, subsequently dismissed from the project.

William Cowen (1791-1864), British landscape painter and printmaker. He left a watercolour painting of the Kensington Canal probably painted from Gunter's bridge in around 1840.

Sir John Rennie (1794-1874), engineer consultant to the failing Kensington Canal Co. He gave a more realistic assessment of the spiralling costs.

Robert Stephenson (1803-1859), engineer became consultant to the building of a railway line along the Kensington Canal, 1844.

Gilbert Abbott à Beckett (1811-1856), humourist and journalist, writer on *The Times* and original *Punch* magazine staffer, like Lord

27

Holland, he was implacably opposed to the Kensington Canal and the railway. He exposed the lumbering project to 10 years of derision in the magazine, so that it gained the soubriquet, 'Punch's Railway'.

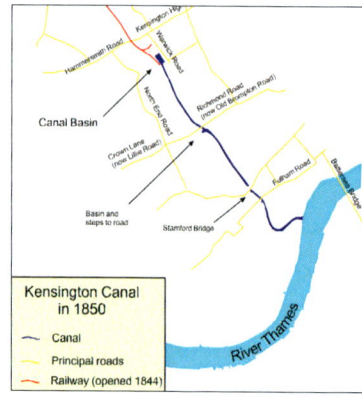

Above: The Kensington Canal layout in 1850

Sir John Fowler (1817-1898), Yorkshireman, civil engineer, creator of the world's first underground railway, the Metropolitan, known for the Forth Rail Bridge in Scotland – a UNESCO World Heritage site – and the Khartoum Railway. He re-built Lillie's bridge over the West London Line in 1860 and designed West Brompton station (Grade II listed) "in the middle of fields" in 1866, next to Brompton Cemetery (1839), (Grade I Listed). In 1868 Fowler presented plans of Richmond Place (North End), along with Bute Street (Brompton) and Edith Grove (Chelsea) to Parliament as part of his 'cut and cover' expansion West of London[5].

Above: Gilbert Abbott à Beckett, circa 1855

Queen Victoria (1819-1901), in her Golden Jubilee Year, visited the American Exhibition and Buffalo Bill's Wild West at the Earl's Court Grounds on 9th May 1887, entering through Richmond Gardens, renamed 'Empress Place' in her honour.

Sir Robert Gunter (1831-1905), grandson of James, was a Crimean War veteran and

Sir John Fowler (1817-1898)

Yorkshire MP. He owned the orchard abutting Richmond (Empress) Place and sold it on to the Metropolitan District Line for their traction maintenance depot. He was also the freeholder of Beaufort House estate in the Enclave.

Joseph Bickley (1835-1923), was a master plasterer specialising in decorative plasterwork and in finishes for rackets and indoor tennis courts. He designed courts at Moreton Morrell and Canford, Hayling Island as well as at Troon and over the 'pond', in New York. In London his work survives at Queen's Club and Hampton Court. He lived at 62 Lillie Road and ran his business from Seagrave Road. He patented a plaster formula that became the mainstay of indoor tennis and Real Tennis courts throughout Britain and in the United States. The particular characteristic of the plaster was that it would withstand damp and condensation. Unfortunately, Bickley died a bankrupt and his formula is lost to us.

Edmonds & Co. (c.1840-1890) purveyors of glasshouses, hot water systems and horticultural factors ran their business from the south side of the bridge approach in Lillie Road. They closed as local market gardens gave way to industrial exploitation. They were replaced by electrical factors, Marsh Bros.

Edward, Prince of Wales (1841-1910) visited the exhibition grounds on several occasions with his entourage. The public house on the corner of Richmond Gardens was named in his honour. It is said that he had assignations with the Jersey actress, Lillie Langtry, in a house along Lillie Road, hence "*the Lillie Arms*" became 'the Lillie Langtry'.

John Graham Chambers (1843-1883) Welshman, Cambridge rowing blue, athlete and an early sports administrator was probably the person most responsible for bringing sport to the Lillie Bridge Grounds in 1865. He codified the 'Queensberry rules' for boxing and was instrumental in the founding of the Amateur Athletics

---

[5] Original preserved at London Metropolitan Archives

Association. The Grounds staged the 1873 FA Cup and were the scene for international wrestling, boxing, cycling, ballooning and athletics. The venue came to an ignominious end on 18 September 1889 when spectators, cheated of a cancelled spectacle they had paid for, staged a riot and burnt down the grandstand.

Above: John Chambers

John Robinson Whitley (1843-1922) a Leeds entrepreneur, opened the 24-acre Earl's Court Exhibition Grounds in 1887, with its entrance in Young's Richmond Gardens. This was after a Roman Catholic prelate had attempted to use the vacant triangle formed by the railway lines for a Catholic school which proved impractical. Whitley, who had met Cody in the USA, raised the capital for his American exhibition and Wild West Spectacle which were followed by French and German shows. Unfortunately, they became a financial flop and this challenging spot had to wait for another entrepreneur to take it on. Incidentally, Whitley was the brother-in-law of Frenchman Louis le Prince, credited as the "father of cinematography".

Above: John Robinson Whitley

William Frederick Cody (1846-1917), known as Buffalo Bill, born in Iowa, was a soldier, bison hunter and showman. He toured the UK and Europe with his Wild West on several occasions in the late 19th-century. He was particular about including First Nation performers in his spectacular presentation. He objected to the term 'show'.

Annie Oakley (1860-1926), born Phoebe Ann Mosey in Ohio, was a famed sharp-shooter and star of Buffalo Bill's Wild West presentation She is said to have been introduced to Queen Victoria personally.

Henry Lovibond, (1840-1910), was a brewer from Clerkenwell who acquired 'The Hermitage' villa and the remnants of its park on the corner of Lillie and North End Roads in 1867, where he built his Cannon's Brewery. In WWI, the premises were taken over by Airco, to construct de Havilland designed aircraft from 1915. After the Hermitage was demolished in the inter-war years, the site was used as a noisy factory for the production of Telfer's Pies.

Above: Cannon's Brewery photo courtesy of Historic England'

The Midland Railway Company established in 1868 its extensive goods and coal yard behind Cannon's brewery and Young's terrace in Lillie Road.

WG Grace (1848-1915) physician and famed amateur cricketer played for the *Gentlemen of the South* and scored a century at the Middlesex County Cricket Club in 1871 while it occupied grounds at Lillie Bridge 1869-72. The turf was not good enough for cricket but other sports thrived there, especially athletics, cycling and ballooning, until the infamous and widely reported riot in 1889 already mentioned.

The Metropolitan District Railway Co. opened its now historic railway traction maintenance workshops in 1872, since known as Lillie Bridge Depot. For details see the Wikipedia entry.

Lillie Road at the turn of the 20th-c. with the entrance to the Midland Railway

Corbett and McClymont, developers and builders of the Gunter estate in Chelsea took over the *North End* brewery in Seagrave Road and installed there a state-of-the-art steam-operated timber works in 1872. They did not stay long and 5 years later moved closer to their development in Chelsea, where they went bankrupt. (They left behind their brick chimney that was taken down in 2016 by the new owners of 1, Seagrave Road).

Movers and Shakers in the Enclave

Above: A wrestling match at the Lillie Bridge Sports Grounds

Above: The once Lillie Bridge Sports Grounds ploughed up in preparation for the 21st century Lillie Square Development, along Seagrave Road. In the background the Fulham Ambulance Station, the Brompton Park residential estate on the site of the former Western Isolation Hospital and the girders of Stamford Bridge, Chelsea FC's football stadium

Above: Entrance to the Lillie Bridge Depot with the barrel-roofed Earls Court 2 Hall in the background, both now demolished

The brewery complex then became Vicker's gin distillery until WWI. It was taken over in 1918 by Sir Robert Burnett's White Satin Gin distillery until 1963 and the breakup of Seagrams. Then part of the premises became the Spaghetti House kitchens. Currently, it is the site of the only commercial winemaker in London, London Cru.

The Metropolitan Asylums Board acquired a 13-acre site at the bottom of Seagrave Road in 1877 to build a hospital and ambulance station. Expansion continued into the 1890s when it became the Western

Above: Entrance to the wine-makers in Seagrave Road

Movers and Shakers in the Enclave

Isolation Hospital, (or Western Fever Hospital) admitting smallpox cases from all over West London. In the 20th c. it became a centre of excellence for treating polio. With the decline of cases, the NHS closed it in 1979 and sold the land for flats. However, the historic London Ambulance Service, the first to use motorised transport has remained.

The London Road Car Company opened its depot for horse-drawn buses on Seagrave Road in 1890. It was one of the largest bus operators in the capital. Henry Royce, an engineer, was already connected with the company in Fulham but actually met Charles Rolls the independent owner of coachworks in Lillie Hall, in Manchester. When horses were finally retired in 1911, LRC became a motorised operation. In the meantime, it was taken over by the London Omnibus Company, which eventually became part of London Transport. It should be mentioned here that on the southern extremity of the Enclave, the last automotive service to close in 2014 was Stewart's garage, a maintenance facility to the London Cab trade at 72 Farm Lane, and now demolished vestige of the huge two-floor stable block of the London Road Car Co., built in 1880.

Above: The ornate rear wall of the former Corbett and McClymont timberworks, Seagrave Road from Merrington Road

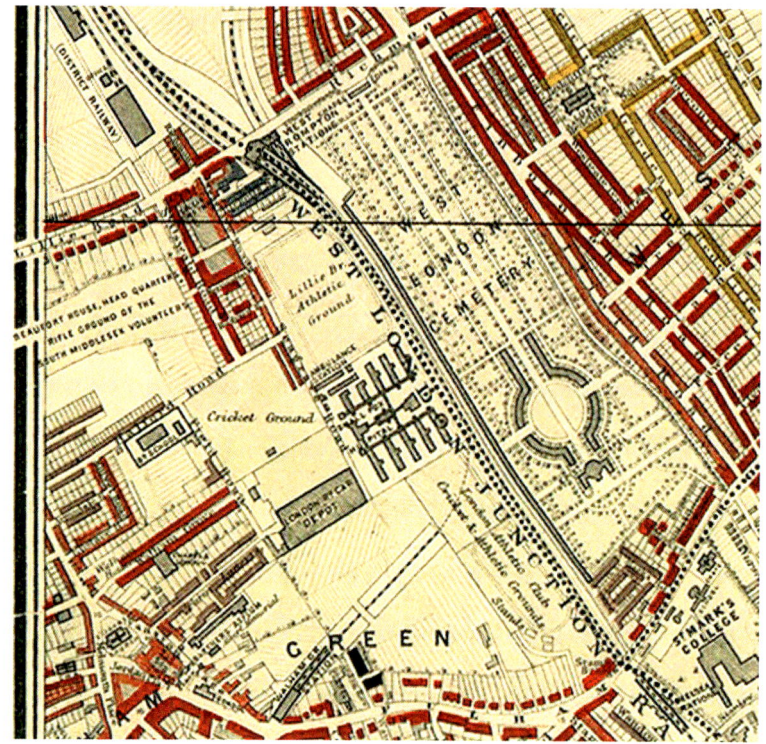

Above: The Western Isolation Hospital, at the centre of Charles Booth's Poverty Map, 1889

Charles Yerkes (1837-1905), was a financier and mass transit pioneer from Chicago, who came to London at the tail end of his life in 1900 and reorganised much of London's underground system. His Piccadilly and Brompton Railway was the precursor of the Piccadilly line whose engineering HQ came to 13 Richmond Gardens (the present 16-18 Empress Place) after his death in 1907. Another American, **C. Howard Crane** (1885-1952), renowned theatrical architect and engineer, would arrive a quarter of a century later in the Enclave from Detroit to erect his iconic Modernist Earls Court Exhibition, completed in 1937.

Above: The Western Isolation Hospital 1870s wall now enclosing the Brompton Park estate and park with public access

Below: LAS - Ambulance Station and Department of Education and Development Fulham in Seagrave Road

Imre Kiralfy (1845-1919) the Hungarian showman and international impresario, rebuilt the 24 acre Earl's Court site, in Mughal style for the Great India exhibition. Later he had the Giant Wheel erected and Empress Hall built by Collard behind Richmond Gardens and Lillie Road in 1894, where he presented musicals and ice spectaculars. During World War I, the Empress Hall was used as an emergency reception centre for thousands of Belgian refugees who sought sanctuary in London as German forces overwhelmed their country.

Charles Féret (1854-1921) Fellow of the Royal Geographical Society, India Office official, editor of the *Fulham Chronicle*, resident of North End (currently called West Kensington, even though it is in fact in Hammersmith & Fulham!) and author of the thousand-page, exhaustive three-volume history of *Fulham, Fulham Old and New*, published by private subscription in 1900. It contains some useful details about the Lillie Enclave but left much to research.

Emmeline Pankhurst (1858-1928), political activist and suffragette, one of too few women on this list, picked the capacious Empress Hall as a venue for one of her well-attended rallies in 1913. She probably did not know at that stage that she would spend eternity just a three hundred yards away in Brompton Cemetery, in the company of other Lillie Enclave movers and shakers, mostly, men naturally.

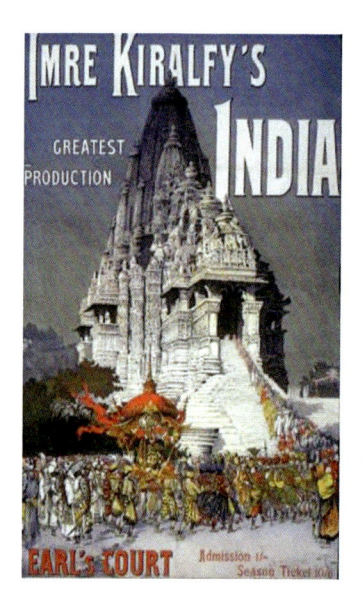

Above, top: India exhibition poster
Above, below: Bassett's Giant Wheel (1894-1907) on the 'Fulham side' in front of Philbeach Gardens with St Cuthbert's church spire visible'

Movers and Shakers in the Enclave

Lord Albert Stanley (né Knattriess) 1st Baron Ashfield (1874-1948), was a British-American businessman, politician and rail transport magnate. He was chairman of the Underground Electric Railways Company of London (UERL) from 1910 to 1933 and chairman of the London Passenger Transport Board (LPTB) from 1933 to 1947. He oversaw the extension of the Piccadilly line from Cockfosters to Uxbridge and likely visited Empress Place on numerous occasions. The dominant structure of Ashfield House at the eastern end of the Lillie Bridge Depot is named in his honour.

Above: American financier Charles Yerkes

The Hon. Charles Rolls (1877-1910) aviator, opened his car showroom in a disused roller-skating rink, the Lillie Hall, in Seagrave Road in 1902, selling French Peugeot and Belgian Minerva sedans. Four years later he formed a partnership with Frederick Henry Royce that became the world-renowned company, Rolls Royce. Their car repair facility lasted there until 1968. Rolls died in a flying accident.

The Three Rs. With Rolls Royce's London depot already established in Seagrave Road, the French Renault company also opened their depot in the street in 1908 and only moved out in 1935. Their place was taken by the Rover Company who continued to service their iconic models, like the Land-Rover, in this spot until 1971.

Above: Mrs Pankhurst under a bit of duress in front of Buckingham Palace

39

The Lillie Enclave, North End, Fulham, London

Above: The former Piccadilly Line HQ at 16-18 Empress Place, on the right. It is subject to a Certificate of Immunity from Listing granted by 'Historic England, with its expiry. date of 19 May 2027. Next to it is the birthplace of musical prodigy, William Hurlstone (1876-1906), 14 Empress Place, originally 12 Richmond Gardens.

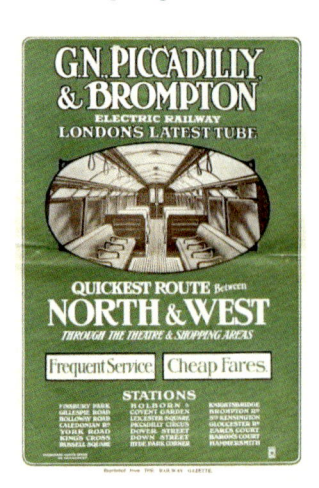

Left: The financier and public servant, Lord Ashfield © NPG

40

Gregory, Bottley & Lloyd (est. 1858 by James Gregory) the second oldest running gem and fossil dealership in the world, moved from Old Church Street, Chelsea and spent 25 years in the Enclave. It occupied 12-13 Rickett Street, off Seagrave Road, 1982-1993 before settling at 13 Seagrave Road until 2007. It is now part of Timeline Auctions in Essex.

Sir Geoffrey de Havilland (1882-1965) engineer, aviator, aircraft designer and businessman began his married life in Baron's Court Road and had his first rented workshop in Bothwell Street, off the Lillie Road in 1909. By 1914 he was employed as a designer by the Air Manufacturing Company (Airco). In the First World War, his skills were put to use in the production of bi-planes by Airco in the space available in Cannon's brewery in the Lillie Enclave. More space was later used for the purpose at the repository of the department store, Waring & Gillow in Hammersmith. The plane parts were taken for assembly in the British Army's Balloon Factory at Farnborough from where they took to the air.

Hans Zimmer (born 1957), later winner of two Oscars and four Grammys, set up a recording studio in 1979 at the bottom of Lillie Yard (a private road). The self-taught German film score composer co-founded the music production

Stanley Myers (1930-1993

Hans Zimmer, double Oscar Winner

company with Stanley Myers, (1930-1993), a prolific British composer of film and TV scores. Their partnership in the analogue era produced the score for the film *My Beautiful Launderette*, among many others. With Myers gone, Zimmer moved to the USA in the 1990s. Zimmer's much-garlanded work is noted for its integration of electronic and ethnic sounds with traditional orchestral arrangements.

Adam Aaronson (born 1956) is a leading British studio glass blower and artist. He established his studio in Rickett Street, off Seagrave Road, in the 1990s and and went on to open the ZeST Gallery on the premises to exhibit other studio glass artists alongside his own work. Redevelopment took precedence over art in this place and the studio and gallery moved away in 2012, to Surrey.

Diana, Princess of Wales (1961-1997), who spent her early years in London in Coleherne Court, just a quarter of a mile up from the Lillie Enclave. On 17 October 1991 she opened the Earls Court 2 extension to the iconic venue. It lasted barely 20 years before falling prey to the then largest regeneration proposal in Europe begun secretively in 2008, under the mayoralty of Boris Johnson.

2012 Olympic venue, Prior to Earls Court playing host to the Volleyball competition at the 2012 London Olympics, the Enclave's Empress Hall was one of 25 venues for the XIV Olympiad held in London in 1948. It hosted the Boxing, Gymnastics, Weightlifting and Wrestling events

Rus in Urbe

The story cannot end without a mention of the flora and fauna that found a haven in this frontier land. In their Ecology Handbook 25 (1993), John Archer and Daniel Keech inform us about Nature Conservation in Hammersmith & Fulham. They write of "two important green corridors associated with watercourses: the River Thames and the Grand Union Canal, once linked by the ill-fated Kensington Canal". If one adds the various network of railway lines and open spaces in the Kensal Green area, another green corridor appears along the West London Line to the Thames. The West London line runs in a shallow cutting along the Borough boundary beside Brompton Cemetery and the now exposed footprint of the former Earls Court exhibition centre. As a result, a variety of habitats could be revived as seen in the 1990s.

Were there the will and commitment from the authorities and the temporary stewards, for such are the owners of this railside land, it could yet be allowed to provide excellent habitat for plants and animals, that is, corridors for natural spread of wildlife.

Today's reader should note that as of 1993 all three green corridors provided, due probably to the presence of some calcareous ballast, an excellent habitat for flora and fauna and the spread of wildlife generally. *Goat willow* and *buddleia* scrub grew amongst sycamores, tall shrubs and grassland. Some of the grassland could still contain species such as *blue fleabane* and *salad burnet*, which are scarce in London, as well as wall lettuce. The wetland along the railway lines at West Brompton station contained huge amounts of *reedmace*, with *water-plantain* and floating *sweet-grass*. It could do so again with an enabling mindset. Further down the down the line, *cotoneaster* and *firethorn* provide plenty of berries for birds and other wildlife ⚜

--- Legacy ---

'The importance of architecture for personal identity and wellbeing is far-reaching and demands an interdisciplinary response.'
Lucy Huskinson, *Architecture and the Mimetic Self*

Nature has its way: Counter's Creek a small hidden tributary of the Thames features in Barton's *'The Lost Rivers of London'*. It became a canal, was corseted into a sewer, filled in, replaced by a railway line, yet still has the ability to flood. For the Lillie Enclave is on the Thames flood plain and is closer to sea level than its neighbour, the Philbeach Conservation Area. The Victorian drainage infrastructure is unlikely to withstand much additional pressure put upon it.

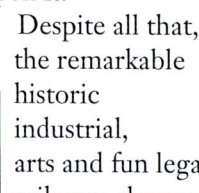

Despite all that, the remarkable historic industrial, arts and fun legacy of the area dwells in the bricks, railways, dozens of film scores, concerts and in the memory of those who have visited, worked, walked and lived in these streets. The Enclave has been a welcoming place for celebrations of national significance, such as the anniversary of the WW2 victory of El Alamein, held at the Empress Hall in 1950, in the presence of wartime leader,

Left: Quietly carrying on their business
Above: Shell carving, copyright of www.londonremembers.com

Legacy

The Empress Hall, Empress Place and the Earls Court Exhibition Centre under construction, 1936 © Historic England.

Winston Churchill, Field Marshal Lord Montgomery and the then Defence Minister, Emmanuel Shinwell MP, representing the Attlee government.

The reader could form the view that the Lillie Enclave has been marked by fiasco and hubris. What that means is that a number of 'interlopers' over time have had their fingers burnt here and lost a lot of money. They either had to cut their losses or seek their fortune elsewhere as did John Whitley, by going to Le Touquet on the northern French coast and turning it into a fashionable resort, where a street is named after him. What remains here in Fulham is the attractiveness of an uncrowded sky for the migratory birds which travel it. Could not the Enclave remain a homage to the elegance and gentility of its built and remarkably diverse heritage? ⚜

The Lillie Enclave, North End, Fulham, London

Above: Earls Court in its shroud 2014
Below: Lillie Yard with the former film music recording studio at the far end

Legacy

Above: The versatile West London Line on the Fulham side of West Brompton station

Left: Gin was distilled in the Enclave, behind Lillie Yard, by Vickers until 1918 when Sir Robert Burnett's White Satin label took over until 1963.

47

The Lillie Enclave, North End, Fulham, London

Above: The former Imperial Arms (1913), a Courage pub at 8 Lillie Road. It displayed the familiar golden rooster logo which was stripped by the developers
Below: Lillie Bridge parish marker stones reversed by masons during recent refurbishment

Legacy

Above: Wetland vestige west of platform 4 at West Brompton station with the rear of the glass blowing studio abutting the chalk downs ballast that hosted the flora and fauna in The Lillie Enclave, 2012

Left: The regrowth after the treatment of the Wetland area in 2018

The Lillie Enclave, North End, Fulham, London

Above: the former Prince of Wales pub
Below: Revival is possible at 16 Lillie Road

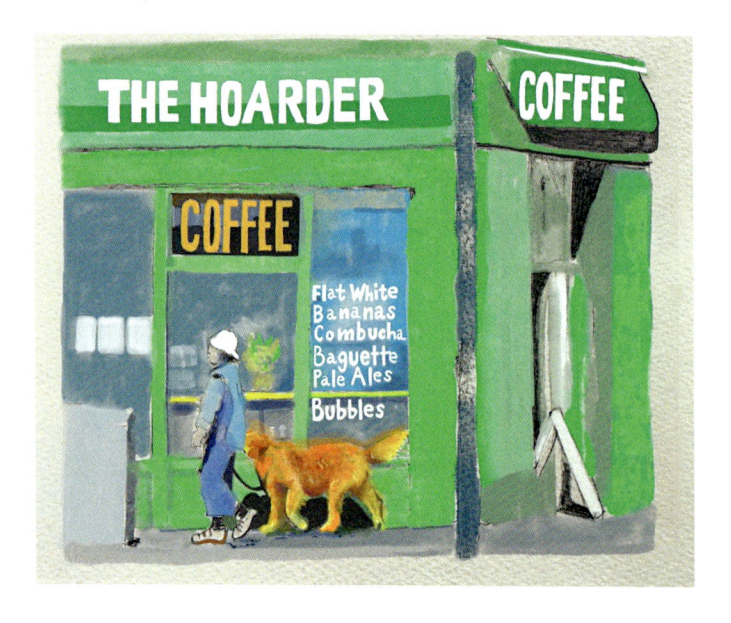

Legacy

Above: The late Earls Court Exhibition Centre and railway verges looking southward Below: The London Oratory School in Seagrave Road

51

Enclave Burials at Brompton Cemetery

- Sir Robert Gunter
- Thomas Crofton Croker
- Sir John Scott Lillie
- William Cowen
- Sir John Fowler
- John Graham Chambers
- Emmeline Pankhurst
- Long Wolf with White Star

Agaricus arvensis in the Enclave 2023

Afterword
by Mark Balaam

The Lillie Enclave is at the heart of the heritage cluster between the historic commercial centre of the North End Road market, the original residential range on the north side of Lillie Road, and the Lillie Langtry pub opposite, the western side of Seagrave Road, the Lillie Road canal bridge, the Grade I and II Listed structures of the Brompton Cemetery and West Brompton station respectively, the Sedlescombe Road, Philbeach and The Billings and Brompton Cutting Conservation Areas. It is also surrounded by/abuts the railway infrastructure of the area.

For many years, since its inception in 1872, Empress Place formed the main access to the Lillie Bridge Depot which in turn served the Metropolitan, District Railway, the Great Northern, Piccadilly and Brompton Railway (GNP&BR) and the London Underground. It is now owned and operated by Transport for London. Just two of the Enclave's original buildings were demolished in Empress Place, at the depot's entrance to make way for the attractive Neo-Georgian structure containing the offices of the already established GNP&BR in 1906.

Immediately to the northwest of the Enclave were the London Midland and Scottish Railway goods yards, used for delivering coal and other goods from the North via the Enclave to West London.

Alongside the Enclave's eastern boundary were more rail exchange sidings as well as access to the London and North Western Railway's goods yards on the south side of Lillie Road. These were used inter alia in two consecutive winters (1898-1900) for stabling the 67 gold and crimson cars of Barnum and Bailey's Circus Train.

The station was strafed by enemy fire during WW2 and a bomb fell on it on the night of 9/10 September 1940, but failed to explode. Despite there being relatively little damage, the West London Line station, on the Enclave side, was closed. Over the next sixty years it fell into an increasingly dilapidated state, with its platform buildings demolished in about 1952, its street level buildings in about 1957 and their supporting beams in the 1970s, after the platform edging stones had been removed in the 1960s.

While the District Line station alongside remained open throughout, the West London Line was used for freight and limited passenger services that for many years only passed through the station site.

Opened on 1st June 1999 by Glenda Jackson MP, then Transport Minister, the station's West London Line platforms were rebuilt to serve two new rail axes. The first was originally operated by Connex between Brighton and Rugby. Southern now plies this route between East Croydon and Watford Junction. North London Railways (later Silverlink) provided local services between Clapham Junction and Willesden Junction. These were extended to Stratford and are now part of the Mildmay Line services within the London Overground network.

These services, alongside the swift resumption of District Line trains at the weekends, have for the last quarter-century transformed West Brompton into a significant interchange, as well as a station that links the Enclave each day with a plethora of centres across London and the South East ⚜

        Mark Balaam
        London, 2024

─────── Acknowledgements ───────

The idea of filling this particular gap in the rich history of Fulham's frontier arose more than a decade ago. I write as one of the settled 'interlopers' in the Lillie Enclave, having grown up in neighbouring Earl's Court, in the shadow of the former iconic exhibition venue.

My memory encompasses the inside of the Empress Hall on an outing to see *Cinderella on Ice*. In its place grew the Empress State Building. At the end of A-Levels our English teacher, Rosemary Cox, invited her class to tea at her house in Lansdown Terrace, 43 Lillie Road, before it and the entire row of genteel Palladian villas gave way to the brutalist *West London Hotel*[7]. Another figure who merits a mention was our history master, Alexander 'Alex' Gamble DSO, (1921-2013) who imparted his passion for the past, imperceptibly at the time, in all its everyday detail.

Many years later, Christine Bayliss, the dedicated head of Hammersmith & Fulham Archives, introduced me to the Borough's photographic collection. Getting to appreciate the area has been enriched by many, among them Angela Dixon founder of the Hammersmith and Fulham Historic Buildings Group, the Enclave natives, Keith Whitehouse and Alex Karmel, and The West London Line Group with its Chairman, Mark Balaam. Friendships and encouragement in the local community have contributed immeasurably to the enjoyment of the Enclave and valuing its hidden heritage, especially, Molly Storck, long-time resident of Lillie Road, and more recently, the wonderful people from 'The Hoarder' at 16 Lillie Road. In addition, I want to thank David Wardrop, late of *Groundwork Fulham*, who alerted me to the exceptional flora and fauna in the Enclave and its watercourse, and for his engaging foreword to this edition.

The written record was made accessible by the helpful staff at the British Library, Fulham Library, Hammersmith Library, the Kensington

Library, the London Metropolitan Archives and the webmasters of London's Lost Hospitals and London Remembers websites.

My gratitude extends to Brenda Dempsey and to Olivia Eisinger and to Hammersmith and Fulham archivist, Annaïg Boyer for their solicitude in the work's production. Particular thanks go to the tireless Anabela Hardwick and Linda Wade, and to Alex Batho of *Countryside Books*, without whom this project could not have come to fruition. Any remaining errors are mine ᛋ

Bibliography

Amies, Chris, *Hammersmith and Fulham Pubs*, The History Press, 2004

Archer, John and Keech, Daniel, *Nature Conservation in Hammersmith & Fulham, Camden*: London Ecology Unit, 1993

Barton, Nicholas, *The Lost Rivers of London*. London: Historical Publications, 1962 and 1992

Brewery History Society, Henry Lovibond & Sons (Fulham) http://breweryhistory.com/wiki/index.php?title=Henry_Lovibond_%26_Son_Ltd_(Fulham)

Bryant, M. A. " John Graham Chambers", *Oxford Dictionary of National Biography*, Oxford University Press, 2004

Cherry, Bridget and Pevsner, Nikolaus, *The Buildings of England. London 3: North West*, Yale University Press, 2002

Corder, Frederick "William Yeates Hurlstone", *Oxford Dictionary of National Biography*, Supplement 1912

Croker, Thomas Crofton, *A Walk from London to Fulham*, William Tegg, 1860, https://www.gutenberg.org/ebooks/29541

Denny, Barbara, *Fulham Past*, London: Historical Publications, 1997

'The Edwardes Estate: Introduction', in *Survey of London: Volume 42, Kensington Square To Earl's Court*, ed. Hermione Hobhouse (London, 1986), British History Online http://www.british-history.ac.uk/survey-london/vol42/pp239-248

Féret, Charles, *Fulham Old and New. London*: Leadenhall Press Ltd. 1900,

AND *Fulham and Hammersmith Historical Society Newsletter*, 15th October meeting. No. 148. Winter 2019. https://fhhs.files.wordpress.com/2019/10/148-winter-2019-final.pdf.

Glanfield, John, *Earl's Court and Olympia - From Buffalo Bill to the Brits*, Stroud: Sutton Publishing Ltd, 2003.

Godwin, George ed. "John Young's obituary", *The Builder Magazine*, 31 March 1877

Higginbotham, Peter, *The Western Fever Hospital, Fulham 2016*, https://www.workhouses.org.uk/MAB-WFever/

William Hurlstone: *Complete Piano Music* – Kenji Fujimura Toccata Classics TOCC0289 2015

William Hurlstone: *Orchestral Works* Lyrita SRCD208 1993 – reissued 2006

'The Kensington Canal, railways and related developments', in *Survey of London: Volume 42, Kensington Square To Earl's Court*, ed. Hermione Hobhouse (London, 1986), British History Online, https://www.british-history.ac.uk/survey-london/vol42/pp322-338

Lillie Bridge Grounds, British Library Evanion Collection, http://www.bl.uk/catalogues/evanion/Results.aspx?SearchType=Heading&ID=174

Lillie, Sir John Scott. *An Historical Sketch of the Origin and Progress of Parliamentary Corruption, and of the evils arising therefrom; in order to prove the ... necessity of parliamentary reform*, London: Effingham Wilson, 1831

Lost Hospitals of London, https://ezitis.myzen.co.uk/alphabeticallist.html

Mitchell, Vic and Smith, Keith, *West London Line – Clapham Junction to Willesden Junction*, Middleton Press, 1996

The Official Report of the Organising Committee for the XIV Olympiad. Published by the Organising Committee for the XIV Olympiad. London, 1948 https://web.archive.org/web/20110727011947/http://www.la84foundation.org/6oic/OfficialReports/1948/OR1948.pdf

Bibliography

Royal Airforce Museum. "de Havilland, Aviation Pioneer", https://www.rafmuseum.org.uk/research/archive-exhibitions/de-havilland-the-man-and-the-company/aviation-pioneer/.

'Sport, ancient and modern: Athletics', in *A History of the County of Middlesex: Volume 2, General*; Ashford, East Bedfont with Hatton, Feltham, Hampton With Hampton Wick, Hanworth, Laleham, Littleton, ed. William Page (London, 1911), British History Online http://www.british-history.ac.uk/vch/middx/vol2/pp301-302.

Tames, Richard, *Earl's Court and Brompton Past*, London: Historical Publications, 2000.

Terry, Francis, in collaboration with 'Create Streets' (2017), "Francis Terry's new proposal for Empress Place, Earl's Court", http://traditionalarchitecturegroup.org/news/2017/10/2/francis-terrys-new-proposal-for-empress-place-earls-court

Vosborough, Matthew, on Hans Zimmer, http://www.muzines.co.uk/articles/yards-ahead/978.

Walford, Edward. 'West Brompton and the South Kensington Museum', in *Old and New London:* Volume 5 (London, 1878), British History Online, https://www.british-history.ac.uk/old-new-london/vol5/pp100-117

Walker, Dave, *'Gigantic: the Earl's Court Wheel'*, (2011), The Library Time Machine. RBKC. https://rbkclocalstudies.wordpress.com/2011/10/27/gigantic/

Wolmar, Christian, *The Subterranean Railway: How the London Underground Was Built and How It Changed the City Forever*. London: Atlantic Books. (2004, revised 2020).

Young, John. *Shopfronts, Porticos and Entrances – A Series of Designs for Shop Fronts, Porticoes and Entrances to Buildings Public and Private*, Taylors Architectural Publishers, 1828, 1843

Index

Aaronson, Adam 15, 41
Abbott à Beckett, Gilbert 27, 28
Airco 15, 31, 41
Amateur Athletics Association 29
Ashfield, Baron Albert Stanley 39–40
  (Né Knattriess)
Ashfield House 39
Atlas Public House 9, 45
Banham Security Ltd. 15, 53
Barnum and Bailey's Circus Train 53
Bartolozzi, Francesco 10, 15
Beaufort House
  Lunatic Asylum 15
Beaufort House School 15
Belgian Carmelite nuns 10, 15
Belgian refugees 11, 38
Bickley, Joseph 15, 16, 29
Biodiversity 11, 43
Birmingham, Bristol and Thames Junction Railway Company,
  see *West London Line*
Booth, Charles 1889 36
  poverty map
Bothwell Street 41
Brompton, village 7, 11, 14
Brompton Cemetery 8, 11, 24, 28, 38
Brompton Park 33, 37
  Crescent estate
Buffalo Bill's Wild West spectacle,
  see *Cody, William*

Burnett's White Satin Gin 15, 34, 47
Canal Bridge 17, 18, 27
Cannon's Brewery 15, 31, 41
Chambers, John Graham 15, 29, 30, 52
Cherry, Bridget 22, 24
Churchill, Winston S, Sir 45
Cody, William Frederick 10, 24, 30
Collard, Allan Ovenden 23
Corbett and McClymont 15, 32, 35
Counter's Creek 11, 12, 14, 32, 43-44
Courage Brewers 48
Cowen William 27, 52
Croker, Thomas Crofton 52
Crane, C. Howard 10, 36
Cutbush, William 27
De Havilland, Sir Geoffrey 15, 31
Diana, Princess of Wales 42
Earl's Court Grounds Ltd.
  see Earls Court
  Pleasure Gardens 5, 15, 23, 30
Earls Court 7, 8, 14, 15, 24, 42, 45-51
Earls Court 2 5, 34, 42
Eastcheap 19, 22
Edmonds & Co. 15, 29
Edward, Prince of Wales 29
Elger, John 21
Empress Hall 10, 15, 23, 38, 44, 45, 55
Empress Place 6, 7, 9, 12, 16, 21, 23-6, 29, 36, 40, 53

60

Index

Empress State Building 5, 15, 23
FA Cup 1873 30
Faulkener, Benjamin Rawlinson 26
Féret, Charles James 26, 38
  (editor, author)
Flood plain 44
Foote, Samuel 12
Fowler, Sir John 15, 28, 45, 52
Fulham and Putney 15
  Orthopaedic Clinic
Fulham Broadway,
  see Walham Green
Fulham Chronicle 38
Fulham Parish 7, 12, 14
Fulham Road 19, 22
Fulham Telephone Exchange 16
Gander & White 15
Giant Ferris Wheel – 15, 38
  Fulham
Godwin, George 20
Gosling, Miss 26
Grace, W.G. 15, 32
Grand Union Canal 14, 43
Great Northern, Piccadilly 15
  and Brompton Line
Gregory, Bottley & Lloyd 15, 41
Gunter, James 26
Gunter, Robert 26
Gunter, Robert Sir, 28, 52
  1st Baronet
Hammersmith Bridge Co. 14
Hermitage, The 12, 14, 31
Hermitage Cottages 14, 26
Hermitage Lodge 15
The Lord Holland, 27
  Henry Richard Vassall Fox,
  3rd Baron Holland

Hurlstone, Martin 24
  Yeates de Galway
Hurlstone, William 15, 24-5, 40
The Imperial Arms 14, 18, 48
  Public House
Indoor rackets courts 29
Jackson, Glenda 54
Kensington Canal 7, 11, 14, 16, 17,
  18, 26-28, 43
Kensington Canal Co. 14, 16, 27
Kensington, Lord, 27
  William Edwardes
Kensington Parish 12
Kiralfy, Imre 10, 15, 38
The Lillie Arms
  Public House, see Lillie Langtry
  Public House
Lillie Bridge 8, 12, 17, 21, 48
Lillie Bridge Depot 15, 16, 23,
  34, 39, 53
Lillie Bridge 14, 16, 23, 30
  (Sports) Grounds
Lillie Hall 16, 33, 35, 39, 41
Lillie, Sir John Scott 7, 12, 13, 52
The Lillie Langtry Public House 14, 18,
  26, 27, 29, 30, 41, 48
Lillie Road 7, 8, 9, 12-16, 21-26, 29,
  31, 36, 41, 50, 53
Lillie Square development 33
Lillie Yard 10, 41, 46
Lillie Yard 10, 41, 46
  (recording studio)
Lockharts Refreshment Rooms 15-6
LAS – London 16, 35, 37
  Ambulance Service
London Black cabs maintenance 35
London Cru 16, 34

61

London Olympics, 2012	42	Railway traction maintenance,	
London Oratory School	7, 9, 16, 51	see *Lillie Depot*	
London Roadcar Co.	16, 34-5	Rennie, Sir John (the younger)	27
London Transport	16, 36	Richmond Gardens,	
Lovibond Henry	15, 31, 57	see *Richmond Place*	
Marsh Bros.	16, 29	Richmond Place,	
Merrington Road	35	see *Empress Place*	
Metropolitan Asylums Board,		Richmond Road,	
see *Western Isolation Hospital*		see *Lillie Road*	
Metropolitan District Line Co.	16, 29, 32-3	Rickett Street	41-2
		Rolls, Charles the Hon.	15, 35, 39
Metropolitan Police Service	16, 32-3	*Rolls Royce*	9, 15, 39
Middlesex County Cricket Club	16, 32	Royce, Sir Frederick Henry	35, 39
Midland Coal & Goods Depot	16, 32	*Royal Marsden Hospital*	20, 22
Ministry of Defence	15, 23	*Royal Tournament*	14
Mocatta, David	20	*Rus in Urbe*	43
Montgomery, Bernard, Field Marshal Lord	45	Seagrave Road	9, 10, 15-17, 29, 32, 34-5 37, 39, 41, 51, 53, 64
Myers, Stanley	41, 42	Shinwell, Emmanuel MP	45
New Cancer Hospital,		Sitting Bull, Sioux Chief	24
see *Royal Marsden Hospital*		*2nd South Middlesex Rifle Volunteers*	16
North End, village	8, 12, 26, 38		
North End Road	5, 12, 31-2	*Spaghetti House*	16, 34
North End Road, market	53	*Stamford Bridge stadium*	33
Oakley, Annie	10, 23, 31	Stephenson, Robert	27
Olympic Games	16, 42	Suffragettes	38
Pankhurst, Emmeline	16, 38-9, 52	*Tanous*	16
Peabody Estate	16	Telephone Place	15, 16
Pevsner, Sir Nikolaus	22, 57	*Telfers* pie factory	16
Philbeach Conservation Area	44, 53	Temperance Movement	15
Piccadilly Line, see Piccadilly and Brompton Line		*Vickers Gin*	16, 34, 47
		Walford, Edward	22, 59
Piccadilly and Brompton Line	36, 39, 54	Walham Green, village	26
Pownall, Frederick Hyde	20	*Watney, Combe & Reid*	9, 15
The Prince of Wales Public House	9, 15, 19, 50	Webb, Joseph	20-23
		Wetland at	43, 49
Queen Victoria	14, 23, 29-9, 31	West Brompton station	

Index

West Brompton station 8, 23, 28-9, 43, 53
West London Line   28, 43, 47, 55
Western Isolation Hospital   16, 33-37
Whitley, John Robinson   15, 30-1, 45

Yerkes, Charles   10, 36
Young & Son, Architects   20-23, 44
Young, John   15, 17, 20, 23
ZeST Gallery   16, 42
Zimmer, Hans Florian   11, 15, 42

Photographic Credits

Anabela Hardwick, Basia Lautman, Linda Wade, Nick Woollven, Alan Godfrey Maps, londonremembers.com (London Remembers), Stephen Richards of Geograph, English Heritage, Hammersmith and Fulham Archives, The Royal College of Music and Britain from Above. Picture on p.54 is entitled 'West Brompton station looking South, August 1933'. Copyright H.C. Casserley.

Above: Will Fulham cats have sills to sit on in the new build, like this one in Seagrave Road?